The Real Deal

Adolescence

Barbara Sheen

Heinemann
LIBRARY

www.heinemann.co.uk/library
Visit our website to find out more information about Heinemann Library books.

To order:

☎ Phone 44 (0) 1865 888112

📄 Send a fax to 44 (0) 1865 314091

💻 Visit the Heinemann bookshop at www.heinemann.co.uk/library to browse our catalogue and order online.

First published in Great Britain by Heinemann Library, Halley Court, Jordan Hill, Oxford OX2 8EJ, part of Harcourt Education.

Heinemann is a registered trademark of Harcourt Education Ltd.

Editorial: Nancy Dickmann
Design: Richard Parker and Tinstar Design Ltd
Illustrations: Darren Lingard
Picture Research: Mica Brancic and Frances Topp
Production: Alison Parsons

Originated by Chroma Graphics
Printed and bound in China by Leo Paper Group

ISBN 978 0 431 90727 7
12 11 10 09 08

10 9 8 7 6 5 4 3 2 1

British Library Cataloguing in Publication Data
Sheen, Barbara.
 Adolescence. - (The real deal)
1. Teenagers - Health and hygiene - Juvenile literature
2. Puberty - Juvenile literature
I. Title
613'.0433

A full catalogue record for this book is available from the British Library.

Acknowledgments
The publishers would like to thank the following for permission to reproduce photographs:
Alamy pp. 11 (Jim Lane), 18 (Dennis MacDonald), 21 (Mary-Kate Denny); Corbis pp. 13 (Zefa/Jon Feingersh [Masterfile]), 14 (Brand X/Rob Melnychuk), 15 (Zefa/Erin Ryan), 16 (Mina Chapman); Getty Images pp. 4 (The Image Bank/Reza Estakhrian), 6 (Taxi/Martin Riedl), 23 (Taxi/Ebby May); Jupiter Images/FoodPix/David Prince p. 27; Masterfile/Jeremy Maude p. 20; Photolibrary.com pp. 5 (PhotoDisc/Geoff Manasse), 9 (Phototake Inc/Pulse Picture Library/CMP Images), 10 (PhotoDisc/SW Productions), 19 (Imagesource Limited), 22 (Fancy), 26 (Workbook, Inc.); Rex Features/Phanie Agency pp. 8, 25; Science Photo Library pp. 12 (Pascal Goetgheluck), 17 (Eye of Science); SuperStock pp. 7 (age fotostock), 24 (Richard Heinzen). SuperStock/ p. 7

Cover photograph of an arrow road sign reproduced with permission of iStockphoto/Nicholas Belton; cover photograph of a skateboarder reproduced with permission of Corbis; cover photograph of a girl leaping reproduced with permission of Rubberball Productions.

The publishers would like to thank Kostadinka Grossmith for her assistance in the preparation of this book.

Every effort has been made to contact copyright holders of any material reproduced in this book. Any omissions will be rectified in subsequent printings if notice is given to the publishers.

Contents

Some words are shown in bold, **like this**. You can find out what they mean by looking in the glossary.

What is adolescence?

Adolescence is the time in life when a person changes from a child to an adult. It is a time of physical and emotional changes. Teenagers are often called adolescents.

The physical process of changing from a child to an adult is called **puberty.** An adolescent's appearance changes on the outside. These changes make adolescents look more like adults. On the inside, physical changes make it possible for young men and women to **reproduce,** or make and have a baby.

Adolescence also brings on emotional changes. These affect the way adolescents feel and act. They affect the way adolescents look at themselves. Adolescents are trying to figure out who they are and how they fit into the world.

All these adolescents are the same age. But only some of them have begun puberty.

Family members often begin puberty at the same age.

When does puberty start?

Puberty starts at different times for different people. Everyone's body clock is different. Puberty in girls usually starts between the ages of 8 and 13. Boys generally enter puberty between the ages of 10 and 15. But it is perfectly normal for puberty to begin later or earlier. Every person is unique. Everyone's body grows and changes at a different pace. Many young people begin puberty at about the same age as their parents or siblings did, but not always. Even twins may begin puberty at different times.

The changes that take place during adolescence can be difficult. Knowing what to expect helps adolescents feel more in control. It helps them get through this confusing and interesting time of life.

Top Tip

Coping with a changing body and changing emotions is challenging and confusing. It is common to wonder if what is happening is normal. Talking with a parent, sibling, or friend who has already been through puberty helps. They can share their experiences with you and tell you what to expect.

Changes for everyone

When puberty starts, the body releases chemicals called **hormones.** They tell the body to start changing. Many of the changes boys and girls go through during puberty are different. However, some changes happen to everyone.

Height and weight

At the start of puberty, adolescents go through a growth spurt. On average, they grow about 7.6–15cm (3–6in) a year for two to three years. The rate and amount of growth can be more or less, depending on the person.

Usually the hands and feet grow first. This can make adolescents feel awkward, but it is only temporary. The body eventually grows enough so that everything is in proportion.

Growth spurts often mean outgrowing your shoes and clothes.

NEWSFLASH

Some young men use illegal hormones called **steroids** to look more muscular. Steroids can damage the liver and heart. They can cause male breast growth and spots. Steroid users often suffer from uncontrollable anger. Some users become **addicted** to steroids.

Growth spurts also cause boys and girls to look more like adults. Girls develop a layer of fat on their breasts and hips. These changes make girls look curvier. Many boys' muscles get thicker. Their shoulders and backs may begin to grow broader.

Growth spurts usually begin earlier in girls than in boys. On average, growth spurts in girls start at about the age of 11 or 12. For boys growth spurts begin about the age of 13 or 14. There is no right time for growth spurts to begin. When growth spurts are finished, most adolescents have reached their adult height.

Adolescents look more like adults than children.

Body hair

Another change boys and girls share is that they start growing hair in new places. **Pubic hair** begins to appear between the legs around the external **sex organs.** Pubic hair is thin at first. As puberty progresses, it gets thicker, darker, and curlier. Hair also grows thicker on the legs and starts to grow under the arms.

Boys may grow hair on their chest, shoulders, and back, but everyone is different. Some boys do not get much hair in these places, while others do. Boys also start to develop facial hair. Many boys start shaving during puberty. Girls may also remove their body hair. Some cultures prefer facial and body hair. Others do not.

Some young men have to shave because their school does not permit facial hair.

Perspiration and oil

Puberty also causes adolescents to perspire, or sweat, more. Body hair traps **perspiration,** and germs on the skin cause a bad smell. Bathing or showering every day or after exercising helps prevent body odour. Adolescents should also use a deodorant or an antiperspirant, and wear clean clothes.

Puberty causes the body to produce excess oil. It can clog the pores, or openings under the skin. This causes spots and **acne.** People with acne have a large number of infected spots.

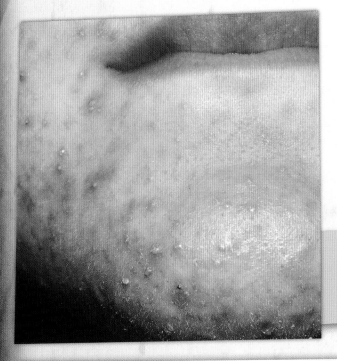

Adolescents can prevent acne by washing their face with a mild soap twice a day and patting it dry. Over-the-counter medicines also help. Squeezing spots can lead to redness and scars. If acne is severe, doctors can prescribe medication for it. Once puberty ends, problems with acne usually lessen.

Almost all teenagers will get spots at some point, but only some suffer from serious acne.

Case Study

Mike had acne. He often rested his face on his hands. This made his acne worse by spreading germs from his hands to his face. Mike's doctor told him to keep his hands off his face. It was hard to do, but it helped reduce the number of Mike's spots.

What happens to girls?

Hormones cause the physical changes of puberty. Boys and girls produce hormones in different amounts. This leads to different physical changes. **Oestrogen** is the hormone that causes most of the changes in girls.

Developing breasts

One of the first visible changes in girls is the appearance of small bumps under the nipples. These bumps are called breast buds. They signal that the breasts are starting to develop. The nipples may start to swell and stick out. The areolas, or circles of dark skin around the nipples, grow bigger. During the growth process, some young women's breasts are painful when touched. As the breasts continue to develop, they become bigger. Sometimes the breasts grow unevenly. This is normal. Over time they usually even out.

Some changes in an adolescent girl's body are clearly visible, while others are not.

Wearing a sports bra helps keep breasts secure and comfortable while you are active.

Staying comfortable

Many adolescent girls start to wear a bra during this time. Wearing a bra is a personal decision. Bras support the breasts and keep them close to the body. Women often feel more comfortable if their breasts are supported in this way.

It takes about three to five years for a young woman's breasts to reach their full size. This process can be longer or shorter. No one can control how long the process takes. Breasts grow into different shapes and sizes unique for each woman. There is no right shape or size for breasts.

Top Tip

Bra sizes have a number and a letter, such as 32A or 36D. The number measures the part of the bra that goes across your chest under your breasts and around your back. The letter measures the cup size, the part of the bra that holds the breasts.

Menstruation

The hormone oestrogen also causes changes in an adolescent girl's internal sex organs. These are the organs involved in reproduction. Once these changes occur, a young woman's first period begins. She can become pregnant and have a baby. **Menstruation** usually begins between the ages of nine and fourteen. However, it can also occur later or earlier.

What's happening?

Every woman has two small, almond-shaped organs called **ovaries** inside her. Each ovary usually contains around 250,000 eggs. They are too small to be seen with the naked eye. About once every month, oestrogen causes one of the ovaries to release an egg. This is called **ovulation**.

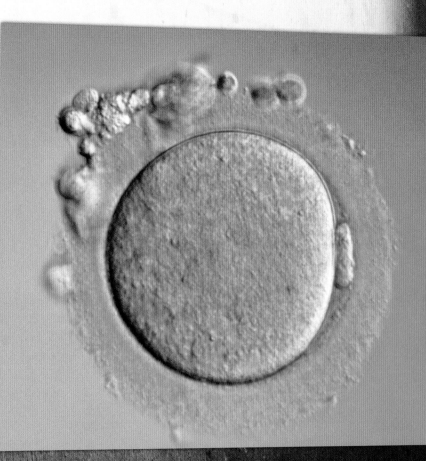

A woman's eggs are too small to see without a microscope.

Once a woman begins to menstruate, she can become pregnant.

During ovulation, the egg travels from the ovary to the **uterus**. It travels through one of two **fallopian tubes** that are attached to the ovaries. Male reproductive cells are called **sperm**. If one of them attaches itself to the egg, it is called **fertilization**. The fertilized egg will attach itself to the wall of the uterus. It develops into a foetus, an unborn baby.

Some time before the egg is released, the uterus makes a special lining of blood and tissues. This lining will nourish the foetus. If the egg is not fertilized, the lining is not needed. It is shed through an opening called the **cervix** and into the **vagina**. Then it exits the body as menstrual blood during a period.

About a year before an adolescent girl begins to menstruate, she may notice a discharge – a sticky, white, odourless fluid that is discharged from her vagina. This is a normal liquid that cleanses the vagina and prepares it for menstruation.

Every girl is different

The **menstrual cycle** is the time between the first day of each period. It is usually 28 to 30 days, but it can be longer or shorter. A girl's menstrual cycle is often irregular for up to two years after her first period. A period can last from two days to one week. Menstrual flow can be light, moderate, or heavy. The amount can change from day to day, and from month to month.

Some women get premenstrual syndrome (PMS) just before each period starts. PMS causes tiredness and moodiness. In some women it also leads to cramps, or pain, in the lower abdomen. A woman may have these problems one month but not the next. Exercising and pain relievers such as ibuprofen help women with PMS.

It is impossible to tell if someone is menstruating by looking at them.

You can continue to play sports during your period. It might even help with cramps.

Menstrual supplies

Menstrual flow is easy to control. Most women use sanitary pads or tampons to protect their clothing. Sanitary pads are placed inside the underpants. Most have adhesive strips that keep them secure. Tampons are inserted into the vagina. They absorb the menstrual flow from inside the body. A string makes tampons easy to remove.

Menstrual blood is odourless. But when it comes into contact with germs outside the body, it can smell. Changing sanitary pads every few hours helps prevent any odours. Tampons should be changed every four to eight hours. They should not be used for longer than eight hours. When tampons are worn for long periods of time, women can develop a deadly disease called toxic shock syndrome (TSS). Using low-absorbency tampons also helps prevent TSS.

Top Tip

Be prepared for your period. If your cycle is regular, keep track of when to expect your period on a calendar. Always carry a tampon or a sanitary pad in your bag or backpack. If you get your period while you are away from home, you will be prepared.

What happens to boys?

Boys change differently from girls. The hormone **testosterone** is responsible for most of these changes. It causes a boy's external sex organs, or genitals, to grow. The **testicles** are the first organs to get bigger. These are the two small, egg-shaped organs that hang behind the **penis**. Their job is to make and store millions of sperm, or male reproductive cells. They must get big before they can do this.

As they grow, the testicles hang lower. One testicle may grow bigger and droop more than the other. This is nothing to worry about. When the testicles are fully developed, they will both be about the same size.

The testicles are delicate. The **scrotum,** a wrinkly sac, protects them. As the scrotum grows, it becomes rougher in texture and darker in colour. The testicles and scrotum usually begin growing when a boy is between the ages of 11 and 16.

Testosterone leads to changes in boys' bodies.

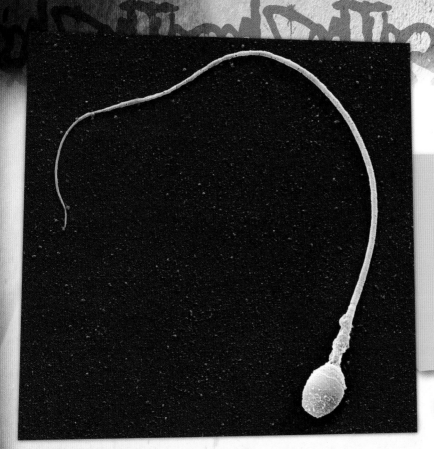

Seen under a microscope, sperm look like tiny tadpoles. This sperm has been magnified about 4,000 times.

Over the next few years, the penis starts to get longer and wider. A man's penis usually reaches its full size by the time he is 16. But all these changes can happen later or earlier. The timing and the size and shape of the penis vary depending on the individual.

Inside the body

Once the testicles are fully developed, they start making sperm. To connect with and fertilize a female egg, sperm must leave the body. Sperm cells travel through a series of tubes that connect the testicles to the penis. In these tubes, sperm mixes with a white fluid called **semen**. When semen passes out of the penis, it is called **ejaculation**.

NEWSFLASH

During adolescence, the brain is still developing. Scientists have found that some adolescents cannot recognize facial expressions that show anger, sadness, or fear as well as adults can. This happens to both boys and girls, but affects boys a little more.

Like their bodies, the voices of girls and boys become more adult during adolescence.

What's happening?

The penis must be erect for a man to ejaculate. Usually the penis is soft and it hangs loosely. When the penis fills with blood, it becomes large, hard, and stands out from the body. This is called an **erection.**

Even before puberty, young boys sometimes get erections. During puberty, testosterone causes adolescents to get erections more frequently. You can get an erection at any time. This happens to every young man, but happens less often to adults.

Sometimes young men get erections and ejaculate while they are sleeping. This is called a **nocturnal emission.** Many adolescent boys ejaculate for the first time during a nocturnal emission. Nocturnal emissions are normal. They happen less often as an adolescent boy moves through puberty.

Other changes

Adolescent boys experience other changes too. In the throat, the larynx grows. It contains the vocal cords. They get thicker and longer. The voice deepens. Some adolescent boys' voices deepen quickly, while others deepen gradually.

An adolescent boy's voice can suddenly crack. It can go from deep to squeaky and back again. This usually lasts for a few months, until the vocal cords develop. Then young men get their permanent adult voices.

As the larynx grows, it begins to stick out from the neck. This causes another change, the development of an Adam's apple. It is a bulge in the front of a man's throat. There is no set time in which these changes occur. Every boy's body is different.

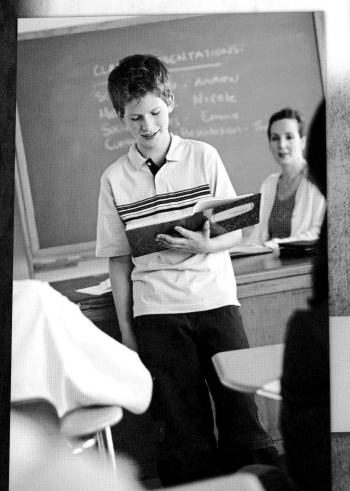

Case Study

Jake had the lead in the school play. A few days before the play opened, Jake's voice started changing. The night of the play, Jake's voice broke during an important scene. Jake felt like running off the stage. But he kept on acting.

It can be embarrassing if your voice cracks in front of your friends, but it happens to everyone.

Emotional changes

Physical changes are not the only changes adolescents experience. Both boys and girls go through many emotional changes too.

Blame it on hormones

During puberty hormone levels rise and fall often. This causes adolescents to feel many different emotions more often and more intensely than ever before. Joy, sadness, embarrassment, anger, and fear are just a few of these emotions.

Shifting hormone levels can cause adolescents to feel overly sensitive. A television advert can bring them to tears. An innocent comment from a friend or family member can make them very angry. Arguments are common during adolescence. **Mood swings** frequently occur. It is not unusual for a teenager to be extremely happy one moment and miserable the next. This emotional see-saw is normal. When puberty ends hormone levels balance out. Emotional ups and downs end too.

Adolescents often feel like they are riding on an emotional roller coaster.

Top Tip

A lot of things can make adolescents angry. A sibling may invade your privacy. Your parents may treat you like a child. A school friend may say something negative about you. If you let your anger get out of control, you might say or do something you later regret. A good way to control anger is to walk away from the situation. Or, take a deep breath and count to ten before responding.

Feeling self-conscious

The physical and emotional changes that adolescents experience can be confusing. They make adolescents look at themselves differently. They feel more self-conscious, especially about the changes to their bodies. Privacy becomes important.

The insecurities some adolescents feel during puberty can sometimes lead to bullying. A person who feels bad about their body may take this out on others by teasing them about the changes that are happening to them. Such bullying can have a very bad effect on a young person's **self-esteem**. It is important to try to understand how other adolescents are feeling during this time of change.

Fitting in

During adolescence, young people sometimes start to ask new questions. They wonder who they are and how they fit into the world. Because they are self-conscious, many adolescents care a lot about what others – especially their **peers** – think of them.

Fitting in with a group and having friends makes people feel good. Sharing feelings and secrets can help adolescents explore who they are and make them feel more secure.

NEWSFLASH

Each day 82,000–99,000 teenagers around the world start smoking. More than 70 percent say that peer pressure is the main reason they started. Smoking is addictive and dangerous. It is the leading cause of preventable death in the United States, United Kingdom, and Australia. It damages the lungs. It causes cancer, heart, lung, and circulatory disease.

Teenagers who smoke often started because of peer pressure.

Peer pressure

Sometimes in an effort to fit in, adolescents make decisions that their friends or schoolmates pressure them into. This is known as **peer pressure.** Peer pressure can be positive. When team mates pressure a team member to practice more, this is good peer pressure. Peer pressure can also be negative. It can lead to dangerous activities such as drinking alcohol, smoking, or using illegal drugs. Saying no to negative peer pressure can be difficult. But it is part of developing your own identity.

Becoming independent

Becoming independent is part of becoming an adult. Sometimes the need to be independent is confusing. Adolescents often want to make decisions for themselves. They may try to handle problems on their own. But they may not know how. They still need help or guidance in many situations. Sometimes an adolescent's need for independence can cause tension at home. Most grown-ups know that becoming an adult is a gradual process. Support and guidance from them helps make the journey to becoming an adult easier.

Teenagers still need adult guidance when making some decisions.

Meeting the challenge

Adolescents face many challenges. Taking steps to cope with these challenges will help you feel more confident.

Coping with intense emotions

Every day, adolescents deal with a wide range of intense emotions. Often their emotions seem to be out of control. Gaining more control over emotions makes people feel better.

Taking a deep breath when you are feeling intense emotions helps you gain control. A change of scenery can also help. Try going for a walk or to the shops, library, or cinema. This gives you a chance to take a step back from a situation or emotion.

Listening to music can help a person calm down.

Top Tip

Keeping a diary is a great way to cope with your emotions. Writing down what is happening in your life gives you a chance to think about and express what you are feeling and why. Talking to someone you trust also helps. Family members, teachers, friends, counsellors, or religious leaders are a few of the people you can turn to.

Feeling insecure

Sometimes adolescents are too hard on themselves and expect too much of themselves. Accepting, and trying to forgive yourself when you do something embarrassing, can be difficult. Remember that your peers are equally worried about how they look to others, including how they look to you, and a lot of what you do goes unnoticed.

One way to help boost your confidence is to think about your strengths. Focusing on your good qualities helps you feel more secure when facing challenging situations.

What do you think?

When people feel good about their appearance, they feel more secure. Because adolescents perspire a lot, many schools require students to shower after physical education classes. Showering helps prevent body odour. Some students feel too self-conscious to shower at school. They say showering in school violates their privacy.

A healthy lifestyle

Living a healthy lifestyle helps adolescents stay positive when meeting the challenges they face. Dealing with intense emotions is tiring. Getting at least eight hours of sleep every night gives people the energy they need each new day.

Eating a nutritious diet helps too. Eating sugary foods such as sweets, soft drinks, and pastries does the opposite. They give the body a short burst of energy that does not last. Once it is gone, the body feels tired and hungry. Caffeinated drinks have a similar effect. They can make people feel nervous and anxious.

Drinking at least eight glasses of water a day is ideal. Water helps flush impurities out of the body. This helps fight acne. Having clearer skin helps adolescents to feel less self-conscious. This makes them more self-confident and better able to deal with the challenges they face.

Exercising or doing yoga relaxes the body and mind.

NEWSFLASH

One out of every five teenagers does not get enough sleep. Changes in hormone levels upset sleep patterns. As a result, adolescents tend to go to bed later. Since school starts early, they sleep less. Lifestyle factors also play a role. Many adolescents are distracted by electronic devices such as computers and televisions in their rooms.

Keeping active

Participating in physical activities is another good way to beat negative emotions. It gives people a chance to release tension and anger in a safe way. Vigorous physical activity also causes the brain to release special chemicals. They give people a feeling of well-being.

Being an adolescent is not easy. There is a lot happening on the inside and outside. Growing up is exciting, but it can also be confusing. Taking care of yourself and knowing yourself helps ease the transition. Remember that what is happening to you is perfectly normal, and you will survive it!

Healthy eating helps you look and feel great.

The female reproductive system

The female reproductive system is made up of several different parts. All of these body parts – including the eggs – are present in a girl's body from the time she is born. However, she cannot get pregnant and have a baby until after puberty.

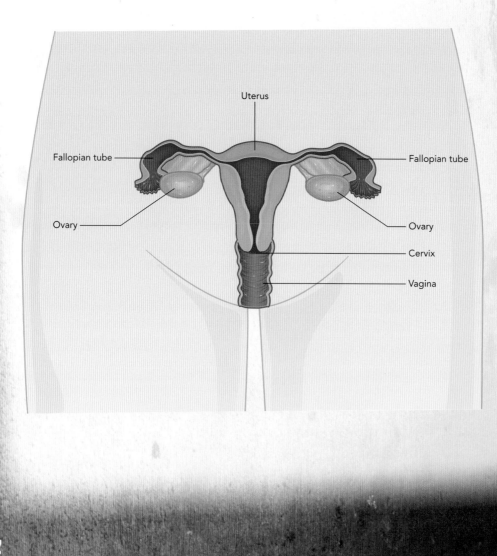

The male reproductive system

Like the female reproductive system, the male reproductive system is also made up of several parts. All of these body parts are present at birth, but during puberty they grow and develop.

Penis

Testicle

Scrotum

Glossary

acne common skin disease that is characterized by spots

addicted dependent on a particular substance

adolescence time of life when a child becomes an adult

cervix narrow passage that leads from the uterus to the vagina

ejaculation release of semen from the penis

erection hardening and enlarging of the penis

fallopian tube one of two tubes that connects the ovaries and uterus

fertilization joining of a male and female reproductive cell to create a new organism

hormone chemical produced by the body that regulates different body functions

menstrual cycle length of time between the first day of each period

menstruation shedding of blood and cells from the uterus lining

mood swing rapid change in emotion

nocturnal emission release of semen during sleep

oestrogen female reproductive hormone

ovaries pair of female sex organs that produce eggs

ovulation release of an egg from an ovary

peer classmate, workmate, or person in the same age group

peer pressure social pressure to behave or look a certain way in order to be accepted by a group

penis male sex organ from which sperm is released from the body

perspiration sweat

puberty time of change in the body that makes it possible for reproduction to occur

pubic hair hair on and around the genitals

reproduce make a baby

scrotum sac that holds the testicles

self-esteem respect for self

semen mixture of sperm and liquid

sex organs parts of the body involved in reproduction

sperm male reproductive cells

steroids hormones that cause the muscles and bones to grow

testicles pair of male sex organs in which sperm is made

testosterone male reproductive hormone

uterus female sex organ in which a foetus grows; also called the womb

vagina female sex organ that connects the cervix to the outer body

Further Resources

Books

The Boy's Guide to Becoming a Teen: Getting Used to Life in Your Changing Body, American Medical Association (Jossey Bass Wiley, 2006)

Girl Stuff: A Survival Guide to Growing Up, Margaret Blackstone and Elissa Haden (Harcourt, 2006)

The Puberty Book: A Guide for Children and Teenagers, Wendy Darvill & Kelsey Powell (Newleaf, 2001)

Websites

Avert
http://www.avert.org/yngindx.htm

Like it is (Australia)
http://www.likeitis.org.au/

Like it is (UK)
http://www.likeitis.org/indexuk.html

Puberty: How Your Body Changes
www.coolnurse.com/puberty.htm

Organizations

Brook Advisory Centres
421 Highgate Studios
53-79 Highgate Road
London NW5 1TL
Telephone: 020 7284 6040
General email: admin@brookcentres.org.uk
Website: www.brook.org.uk/content/

Telephone Helplines

Childline   0800 11 11
SEXWISE   0800 28 29 30

Index